GAIL CLOUD

THERAPIST'S DAUGHTER

A MEMOIR IN VERSE

Copyright © 2024 by Gail Cloud. All rights reserved. Thank you for complying with international copyright laws by not scanning, reproducing, or distributing any part of this book in any form without permission, except in the case of brief quotations included in articles and reviews. For information, address Permissions@CitrinePublishing.com. The views expressed in this work are solely those of the author and do not necessarily reflect the views of the publisher.

This is a work of nonfiction. Nonetheless, some names, identifying details, and personal characteristics of the individuals involved have been changed. The author of this book does not dispense medical advice or prescribe the use of any technique as a form of treatment for physical, emotional, or medical problems without the advice of a physician, either directly or indirectly. The intent of the author is only to offer information of a general nature to help you in your quest for well-being. In the event you use any of the information in the book for yourself, which is your constitutional right, the author and publisher assume no responsibility for your actions.

This book is printed on partially recycled paper with ink that does not contain animal byproducts.

Editing: Melissa Kale · Cover Design: Rolf Busch · Interior Design: Hammad Khalid
Cover: Dancer by Edwin Tan · Shadow by Robin Beckham · Therapist by Pavel Danilyuk
Interior illustration by Darya Kuznetsova, Vecteezy.com · Photos reprinted with permission

Library of Congress Cataloging-in-Publication Data

Cloud, Gail

Therapist's Daughter: A Memoir in Verse

p. cm.

Paperback ISBN: 978-1-947708-09-9

Ebook ISBN: 978-1-947708-99-0

Library of Congress Control Number: 2024905707

First Edition, July 2024

 CITRINE PUBLISHING

State College, Pennsylvania, USA

(828) 585-7030 · www.CitrinePublishing.com

For information about special discounts for group purchases,
please call (828) 585-7030 or email Info@CitrinePublishing.com.

PRAISE FOR
THERAPIST'S DAUGHTER

"'TheRapist's Daughter' is how I choose to misread the title of Gail Cloud's unique memoir, written in semi-poetic style of the Greek classics. Her odyssey begins with her lifelong love of dancing which her father dismissed as 'showing off.' The reader watches her dance her way past complicated emotional roadblocks, increasingly creative, determined, graceful, and wise."

—Susan Margolis Balk
Founding Director of HateBrakers
Retired Columbia University Professor and Former Literary Editor at *Playboy*

"Touching and courageous, *Therapist's Daughter* is an inspiration for all who choose to see our childhoods clearly. In seeing her father's 'warts and all', and yet finding the underlying love for him in poems, Gail Cloud breaks a generational chain and beckons us to do the same. In 'Possibilites' she writes, 'Why in the world would I base (who and what I want to be) on what once was?' Good question! What I find for myself is that this is a process with no end. The past keeps being reworked—and this volume opens a creative portal in that process."

—Clifford Passen, MD
Child and Adolescent Psychiatrist

"I was so moved by this book. Gail Cloud eloquently illustrates the process of awakening to childhood trauma and her path towards healing. Though stories may differ, readers will no doubt see themselves reflected in this lyrical process of heartbreak and individuation."

—Sarah Buino
Creator of *Conversations with a Wounded Healer*
and Author of *The Ordinary Trauma Project*

"With unapologetic honesty, *Therapist's Daughter* bares one woman's soul to the world, sharing moments of vulnerability, pain, joy, and gratitude. The sense of intimacy is palpable, as if the author were confiding in us about her life's trials and its joys. Gail Cloud's storytelling encapsulates a myriad of human emotions—making us laugh, cry, and contemplate the meanings of life, family heartache, love, loss, and identity. Her raw, unfiltered emotions offer us a glimpse into the complex world of human experience."

—Marie O'Neill
Author of *And the Lotus Opened: A Memoir*
and Founder of Padma Life Coaching

TRIBUTE

As with any large, important endeavor, there is no way I could complete this vulnerable task without many important people supporting me along the way.

First and foremost, to my husband, who stood by me throughout my process, all the while wondering when I could let this go. Yet, he was the first one I read my poems to and who heard iterations of my memoir.

To my sister, who was part of my process and had to experience the effects of my poems while they stirred up her own memories. She is part of the fabric of this memoir.

To Susan Balk, who was invaluable to me in being an ear and eye, sensitively reading and encouraging my writing, and slowly teaching me how to write and bring the audience into the room.

To Melissa Kale, whose expertise and sensitivity in editing helped me with the whole process, which has been completely new to me.

To Penelope, my publisher, whose exquisite sensitivity to my experiences was invaluable in helping me to birth this project.

To the many people I interviewed to get their sense of this person with whom our lives intersected, who helped me to see him from their own lenses.

And last but not least, to my family members, past and present, who were greatly part of this whole experience, each in their own way.

Thank you for helping me to bring my experiences to life, not only for me but to help others who know intimately what it is like to be lied to, taken over, and to lose a part of themselves to another, and how to reclaim their lives.

TABLE OF CONTENTS

Dear Reader IX

Therapist's Daughter XI

HIM

Breakfast with My Father 15

From Peasant Stock 17

My Father 19

Into the Room 21

Like the Pied Piper 25

Passover 27

Had Been Had 33

Candy Pants Hands 35

Take Me Out to the Ballgame 37

ME

A Demon Inside Me 43

Then I Started to Dance 45

My Mom 51

My Bubbe 53

Climbing a Mountain: A Hero's Journey 55

Blind 61

Lied To 63

Memories 65

COMING UNDONE

Naïve 69
On the Surface 71
White Collar Crimes 73
The Lost Carny 75
From Behind the Curtain 77
Forgive 79
Coming Undone 81
Losing His Mind 85
Off the Hook 87
The Master of Projection 89

MY DANCE

Independance 93
First Romantic Love: Saga 95
Endings and Beginnings 103
My Individuation 105
Motherhood 107
Marriage Number Two 109
Transcendance 111
Tribute 113
Possibilities 115

EPILOGUE

What a Picture Is Worth 117
Revisiting My First Love 127
Dance Is Life 131

About the Author 133

DEAR READER

In sitting and thinking about this book—
About what I lived, experienced, and took,
I realize the importance of story.
To pass down to generations for entertainment and for learning.
To know about our families and from what and where we come.
And yet sometimes we get caught in the stories
As fraught and yet enticing as morning glories.
So to separate the wheat from the chaff,
To own ourselves including our gaffs.
To know and to keep what is us and ours,
And to leave with the past that which is theirs.
That is the true legacy for our heirs.

For you, my reader—
Stories are important.
Tell your story.
Enjoy your journey to disentangle
And share, share, share
As gently as you would hold an affair to your breast,
Holding it gently and firmly against your chest.
Sharing is a heartfelt way of expressing your caring,
As completely integral and innate as your bearing.
So share your soul stories whether through whisper or bellow
And continue the line for your own generations to follow.

In trying to get my own lens clear,
I keep in mind that memory has a way of being illusive.
It is not conducive to knowing the truth of what actually occurred.
So in peering through my looking glass of the past,
These stories I have amassed
Are through my eyes alone
And at times may seem overblown.

THERAPIST'S DAUGHTER

I am a therapist's daughter. Growing up in Topeka, Kansas, near what was then one of the best psychiatric schools and hospitals in America, I thought all fathers were psychiatrists. In our small neighborhood, most of the fathers attended Meningers, where they were studying to be some form of mental health practitioner.

As I grew up, I discovered that children of psychiatrists truly share familiar experiences. We know what it is like to be a type of guinea pig in our own homes. This book is about my experience. My father used to say, "Therapists really are rapists, such the name—the rapist."

What a concept, and what a way for a therapist to see himself. I believe he meant that a therapist goes in and helps to investigate a patient's unconscious, his sense of it being a great invasion of the person's psyche.

Such is the experience I had with my father, a great invader.

PART ONE:
HIM

BREAKFAST WITH MY FATHER

When we were little, it was banana pancakes
And what dad called garbage—
Finding leftovers in the fridge, mostly red salami and cheese,
And scrambling them together.
But Sunday breakfast was special.
We ate and we talked and we laughed and we walked.
Banana pancakes and dad talking—and he could talk—
Was all that we could want.

As soon as we could hike and bike to some fun adventure,
Excursions were our delight—
To parks and through parks no matter the weather,
We hiked and we biked to one place or another.
Sometimes it was only to our local deli
For orange lox and cream cheese with bagels and pastry.
We walked and we talked as we moved with our treasure.
To our favorite place for bagels with dad was pure pleasure.

Sundays with no pleading.
Mom, with her head under the covers, got to sleep in,
And we could be what he called us, breakfast clubbers,
With dad as our leader and our djinn.

As we got older, mom joined us for brunch.
We explored different places; we were quite a bunch.
We sat around the table with dad at the head.
He spoke of all of the stories he lived.
He spoke of baseball and his time as a player.

He spoke his ideas and of parents he couldn't forgive,
Those parents who, with him, had no prayer.
He spoke of his life, his hates and his loves.
He spoke of the navy, his exploits and his dates.
He spoke of his Zaydie, who he loved with a passion.
He spoke of his Uncle, who was his role model.
Wooing his son and his daughters he coddled,
Dressed all in black and grey and no interest in fashion,
Disallowing us, his daughters,
To do our hair and makeup and play with what we wear.
But sports and my brother were another matter;
He had plenty of time off work to coach and to blather.
There were no questions about our thoughts and our interests,
And when I would bring something up,
He would change the subject matter
To talk about his inquests and himself, a constant prattler.

To us, this was dad; this was breakfast; this, to me, was normal.
It never occurred to me it could be any other way, so, then,
I really had no quarrel.
But breakfast was great.
It was time with dad
For pancakes and steaks, for bagels and plates,
For life stories and fun and food and just plain breakfast with dad.
That is all I knew.

FROM PEASANT STOCK

The only son from a peasant on his mom's side
And a bookbinder for Kings on his dad's.
At least, that is what he says.
His name was Roy.
His game was a ploy.
He became a therapist—as he said, "the rapist."
He raped people's minds while he said, "Just be true."
As he extolled being blind, "Hey, I'm Mr. Magoo."

He would say to us—jokingly?—
"I'm no par-King; I'm King of the World;
I'm Mr. Magoo; isn't that a whirl?"

He hated his mother,
His work den a womb as dark as a tomb.
Secretly wishing he had breasts
To smother with and caress.

He was full of word games and puns.
Trust was his name,
Freedom his game.
"Go fly free," he might say,
"But stay, oh please stay.

I want to be true, and I love stumbling around,
Just call me Mr. Magoo; Just call me Mr. Magoo."

Mr. Magoo is a cartoon charater who was almost blind, wearing thick glasses and stumbling around, bumping into things in his blindness. My father likened himself to Mr. Magoo because he thought it was a good thing to be stumbling around in the dark. He always said, "Mr. Magoo is my role model."

MY FATHER

Lover of puppy dogs and babies,
Fairy Tales and Tall Tales,
Innocent women and children.
The Savior and little boy and charming the rapist (therapist),
    Reading Fairy Tales,
    Telling Tall Tales,
Winding me around his crooked thumb,
Telling stories of being a bum,
    Admitting his cruelty
        To which I chose not to believe
        Until I saw it clearly.
Afraid of the darkness,
Scared of loud noises,
Waiting in the dark of night
As my knight Don Quixote
Came into my room...

Nightmares, puppy dog tails,
Tales of fancy,
    Life Tales.

Tales of Truth, tales of lies,
Words of love,
    Puppy dog hugs—
My father.

INTO THE ROOM

It was dark in my room,
Sleeping on my belly in
   the middle of my bed,
Pulling up my sheets
   and over my head.
Sniffing my scent made
   me feel safe,
And at the time,
   I was only a little waif
of 3 or 4
When dad walks in,
And soon I find
   I was misled.
I thought he came in
   to soothe,
But he had something else in his mind to prove.
To talk with me I thought.
Today was one where I got mad again.
It was easy for me to get overwrought.
I got mad easily cause I was really so hurt.
Mom was distant and my sister wasn't my friend.

He sits beside me upon my bed.
I place my head upon his lap
For him to comfort me and stroke my head.
It never occurs to me he has other ideas instead.

He begins to tell me I need to use my words,
And that he is uncomfortable with me retreating.
I thought I was only taking time and space for me,

So this makes me feel I—or something—is wrong.
He says, "Life can be so fleeting.
Come to me and come into my mind.
I will make sure I treat you kind.
You can't shut out life and go so deep,
And so far away from me you sleep."

I am confused.
What is it he really means?
What happens if I refuse?
And then he strokes my hair.

A feeling surfaces I don't understand.
It feels so good it is hard for me to bear.
What, if anything, should I beware?
It feels so good though.
It is setting my skin aglow.
I don't want to lose this feeling.
Will he leave if I don't give in?
This, to me, feels both bad and healing.
He is my father and the one who I trust.
Am I retreating into myself, and is that bad?
So I guess to go into him I must.

So in I give.
I gave him my mind and my soul.
It took me many years to then retrieve
And to give myself reprieve.

This is something that has been hard for me to forgive
And hard for me to understand,
Until I later realized it was my right.
I wasn't getting lost inside myself as my dad told me.
I was taking up space to be myself,
Something for which I had to fight.

Dad must have felt lonely,
So he found a way to hold onto
A very young girl who was drawn to and trusted
Her only dad.

LIKE THE PIED PIPER

Like the Pied Piper, we knew
He had all the answers.

With the force of his charisma, we believed him.
With the force of his charisma, we followed him.

Like the Pied Piper,
He had all the answers.

"What I say is good and true;
Listen to me as I see you through and through.
I have all the words and I know what is right,
So only defy me if you want a fight."

Like the Pied Piper, we knew
He had all the answers.

"Listen to me. I know the truth.
And I knew better than my parents,
Even in my youth.

I knew better than my teachers.
I knew better than my bosses.
Listen to me. I know all the answers."

So we listened to him
And believed all his answers.
We believed his stories and let them romance us.

Like the Pied Piper,
He had all the answers.

And then one day when we were grown,
We knew,
It is not what we say that is true.
It is shown by what we do.

We see the truth through our actions.
We don't see them through our attractions.
We knew: He might be the Pied Piper,
But he doesn't have answers.

We had become lost in his words,
So we listened to what was said as if it were true
And not what we do.

No more are we gullible.
This is not at all discussable.

The truth is shown, not by our hearing.
The truth is shown, most by our seeing.

"I'm the Pied Piper.
Listen to me; I tell the truth,
And the truth will set you free."

"No more," we say, "no more can you fool me.
We know the truth—that we guarantee.
It is shown by what we see, and we now see thee."

PASSOVER

It was a time to gather for a ritual of Jewish remembrance
Of a time when we were enslaved by the Egyptians,
And made our Great Exodus across the Red Sea to be saved.
This, the only day dad celebrated being a Jew,
Was truly his day, with endless words of his to say.
He knew he had to prepare,
So he would be ready to share,
Knowing how much his Zaydie,
His little Hasidic grandfather he revered,
Would very much care.
In his day, family bowed to Zaydie,
And he led the whole service with his favorites,
Dad at his one side and his cousin on the other,
As he read and he sang and he chanted,
The men at one table and the women and children at another.
Dad's grandfather he loved wholeheartedly
And never did take for granted
That little old man
Who I heard was hated by many and loved only a few.
Dad was one he loved, and who was I to argue?

People came over just before sundown,
Came from all over the town,
Patients, friends, and family
Even overcoming some days of torrential rain,
Never even trying their enthusiasm to restrain
To come to this event—
Muslim, Christian, Buddhist, agnostic, and Jew—
Where dad greeted us all at the door, one and all,

Everyone, or I should say, me too, excited for all that was in store.
He greeted us all dressed in black like his Zaydie
With hugs, and to me, that made me feel special,
As if I was the one by dad's side as he was his Zaydie,
And I felt in my heart a very strong tug.

We gathered in the living room with rented tables filling the space,
Soon all of us sitting around it, giving the room grace.
The table set with more dinnerware than at Thanksgiving,
Waiting for dad to start telling the fable.
We all, and I, waited with bated breath,
And it felt to me as strong as life and death.
For what he would say all about each and every one of us there,
One by one, he singled out to say
Words that I longed for, just as everyone else did that day.
To hear how he felt and what I meant to him,
As powerful a wanting inside me as a hymn.
It was this day and this day alone
When he spoke to me of my meaning, especially to him.
It took sometimes an hour to do so with all at the table
Before he came out of his trance and started going through the service.
Most came only to listen to him, their guru, perform
As he remembered and attempted to channel his little Zaydie,
Whom he adored with us as his witness.

Telling the tale from the time of Exodus,
Argue he must and at times, made quite a fuss
Of words like hope and freedom and even forgiveness.

We all read along,
Happy to be a part and to belong
To a celebration with those worldwide.
We read with such pride,
Proud we no longer have to hide.

There to listen to dad, to help, and to discuss
Concepts like hope and freedom,
Which is now our right and our very kingdom.
Dad was adverse to hope, thinking it led folks astray
And left them really in more disarray.

Dad never did believe in forgiveness,
Believing it would take away from us and not give to us.
The Egyptians and his parents he did curse,
Not even shedding a tear in sadness
For the plagues that befell them,
Never letting anything or anyone his beliefs to disperse.
And me, sitting there wanting desperately to believe,
Often left very confused
If I didn't believe what he was saying.
Are my thoughts wrong and can they be proved?
What does it mean when I don't agree?
Am I bad? Am I wrong? Do I have a right to be me?

Then it was time to eat and to dine,
Which in the old days, we did recline
With fish and matzah, maror and lamb shank.
We talked and we ate and we supped and we drank.

Dad ended the service
With another lively discussion of purpose.
He offered for us to tell our own story
Of our journey to freedom that year,
But he went first, and he talked forever
Of his journey,
Which was most painful and always a difficult endeavor.
No one else there could even come near his eloquence.
I occasionally shared,
A compulsion to do so I felt so inwardly intense,
To please my dad and share my grief.
But as I grew older and bolder,
I left it to the others, much to my relief.

Many stayed to share
And to openly bare
Their journeys which were truly as sacred as prayer.

When the evening was over,
Dad thought he had failed
To give us the meaning his Zaydie unveiled.
In truth, he really did succeed to share with us its creed.

But instead of being about us and those of us around the world,
It was about him and his beliefs, openly unfurled.
And this service of Passover, where we survived and escaped
As plagues passed us over,
Was only about him, for there was no other.
His closeness with Zaydie, his anger with his dad,
And his inability to forgive,
Which he repeatedly relived.

But Passover stays with me,
And I celebrate it to this day,
To share with family and friends and to all about whom I care.
This story of love and hope and persecution and freedom
Was a gift from my dad.
I follow the ritual and make it my own,
No longer doubting myself and my agency,
For really, he succeeded, and it is my right and my kingdom.

HAD BEEN HAD

And then one day it came to pass;
This happened to be at Christ-mas.
There in our Jewish stockings
Was something that was very shocking—
A package of life-sized red licorice candy pants.

Yes, candy pants, and I looked at it aghast.
Do I put them on?
Was this a con?
Where was mom?
Did she get one too?
And, are they something to eat?
To do so would be quite a feat.
I looked at my sisters, confused and a bit scared
as we registered their meaning.
We just stood for a minute and stared.
I was only twelve.
They aren't for us.
They are for my dad.
This was hard to take in.
I should be extremely mad.
Had I been had?
Could he be this bad of a cad?
I asked, "Why are you giving these to us?
What were you thinking?"
As I had no inkling.
And for once, this man of many words had none;
But it was from my dad.
It was.

CANDY PANTS HANDS

Behind the scenes, he pulls the strings with sticky hands,
And he gives us red licorice candy pants.

Sticky and sweet,
"Don't leave me," is the message he expresses,
As sticky as his caresses.

He says, "Go fly.
Follow your dreams,"

And holds me with his sticky candy pants hands.

"Find your mate and propagate.

Live your life in truth," which I can't dispute.
Yet, dad, you lie, disguising the truth with a toothpick in your tooth,

And he holds me with his sticky candy pants hands.

"Speak the truth;
Follow your passion,

And come home to me," is his message.
"I'll take care of you and be your god
And hold you to me with my sticky candy pants hands."

Until one day I say to him inside my mind, *Set me free*.
Then I find my voice; I find my passion; I find my truth.
With my truth, he hasn't the control he had in my youth.
And his sticky hands let go as he flees.

TAKE ME OUT TO THE BALLGAME

Take me out to the ballgame.

"I love baseball," he would say.
"When I was growing up, I played all day.

I was 7, not 11,
And took the El by myself
To see the Cubs play.
I guess you could say it was kind of a hub.
I snuck in and climbed the fence
So I could see the offense and defense.
It cost me a dime and the money was mine.
I came home in time for dinner.
My parents dinner was put on a simmer.
They never asked me where I was.
It didn't matter, I was so buzzed."

Take me out to the ballgame.

"Then I was a teenager.
I really wanted to play in the majors.
Although I could run
And in the infield I got things done,
In the end, I was too small,
Even though I could really throw the ball.
Then I tore the ligaments in my thumb,
Which made me feel so awful glum.
It put an end to my baseball career

And made my dreams disappear,
So I decided to become a bum or a..."

Take me out to the ballgame.

"Later I became a father,
Never ever ever a bother.
I wanted eight children
To hold inside me like brethren.
To field a ball game—
That was my dream.
My wife, Arlene, was not into that scheme."

Take me out to the ballgame.

"When I had my son,
My coaching then had just begun.
I used my knowledge and skill
To take the team and drill and drill.
To become one of the best,
I won many of their tests.
They became the champions
With me as their captain."

Take me out to the ballgame.

"Baseball is my game.
It is so much like life,
Even with all the strife.

I was so in love with it,
It never occurred to me
That to my girls it didn't fit.
The girls were left behind.
To them, I was extremely blind.
I could go on and on

But

Baseball is my game."
Take me out to the ballgame.

"Baseball is like life.
It is both exciting and full of strife.
In the game, you can hit, steal, and run.
Yes, it is so much fun.
There are also rules you are supposed to follow.
The key is knowing when.
And it is not about getting even.
It's not that you have to obey.
There are many ways to break the rules and still not go astray.
That is the art and skill of the game.
You even get to run and throw people out on base or at home.
And while you do, you hear others shout.
Ah, what a game.
Baseball is like life. I can talk about this forever."

Take me out to the ballgame.

PART TWO:
ME

A DEMON INSIDE ME

When I was little,
You could say I was brittle.
I was sure I had a demon within me.
It was hidden deep in my psyche.

Angry I got.
Sad I was not
As I loudly exclaimed
Why it was I was so distraught.

My brother and one sister
Had trouble with my blister,
From him I received.
A door sign that said,
"Please don't interrupt me.
I am having a temper tantrum."
Maybe they would have preferred I be in an asylum.

Dancing saved me.
It gave me an outlet.
It offset my internal upset.
My sister had none,
So jealous she did become.
She handled it with food,
And afterwards, would listen to music and brood.
So she was put on a diet,
And she chose to be quiet.

I was labeled the difficult one.

To them, I was selfish.
I felt they treated me like rubbish,
Never bothering to see what I really accomplished.

It didn't help that dad was adept
At keeping us wanting and at a distance,
Which was where we all had little resistance.
He walked into a room and took all the air.
We were then all alone, each with our despair.

So inside, I had what I called a demon.
What was it really, but loneliness and anger—
That's how I felt, all alone in my chamber.

THEN I STARTED TO DANCE

When I started to dance, I really was taking a chance.
Never before had it even been a thought.
It must have lived deep within my soul,
Just waiting for a time for it to show me its seed,
And for that, I was in deep need.
I was 9 at the time.
I saw a movie of a ballet class on TV on a random Sunday afternoon,
Snuggled up in the white coverlet of mom and dad's bed.
It spoke to me deeply like nothing else had.
I came alive inside.
It was a class of young dancers.
For me, it held important answers.
Running downstairs to find mom in the pink kitchen,
With her short dark hair, sitting with her legs crossed,
Smoking a cigarette,
Taking a much-needed break from us, her four kids.
I started the following week,
And when I was older,
I remembered her speaking of her early thwarted desire to dance,
So she did recognize my fire.
Her parents had her playing piano,
Which wasn't her choice and which she didn't seek.
This was truly a rare gift from my mom, as she did it for my sake.
I knew she asked her friend who was a ballet dancer from whom
I should take.

She drove me silently to my lessons while smoking and stressed,
And dad later made fun of our passing gasses,
As he sometimes came early and watched my classes.

While at my performances, he waved and applauded,
As if he were the one who was being lauded.
But mom got me started, and at times, with me, was silently impressed.

Dance took me away from the grasp of my father's loving trap.
Dad loved his sports,
And dance was not something he could support.
It looked to him like showing off,
So it was something at which he could easily scoff.
Don't dance around me; I don't want to see.
For then I would be tempted, don't you see?
Might be something he thought,
And something part of me bought,
But dance speaks to my soul and that is a feeling I can't control.

I began as a novice.
The structure it provided me I sorely needed.
I remember walking down the steep stairs to see a room
        enclosed by French doors,
Quietly opening them to see girls like me
Doing exercises on a large wooden floor.

The back of the room was enclosed by glass doors.
I remember I couldn't wait to get into class.
I went to the dressing room to change into my leotard and tights.
Black and pink were required to wear,
And I put them on and felt so right.

I took to dance like a duck does to water.
For me it wasn't easy, but I loved it intensely.
The discipline filled my need immensely.
At a loss, in a home with little rules,

Learning the movements that made me feel strong,
I sincerely heeded.

I held myself and my muscles so tight,
But my mind was quite able and bright.
As I tried and I learned and I repeated over and over the steps,
Moving from the barre to the dance floor, and I leapt and I leapt,
Happily in another world where my soul felt free.

I started slowly, only one class a week.
By the time I was twelve, it became every day.
Hours a day I spent, and each exercise I tweaked
Until eventually, I began to notice my body take shape,
And I began to feel upon perfecting my technique,
How I could fly inside,
Which was a thrill and brought me a spiritual mystique.

When my movements were controlled,
When my muscles became supple,
I was able to let the movements flow through me,
And I felt myself becoming strong and fluid and bold.

My teacher was a long loose-limbed man with a balding head.
He saw me and nurtured me,
And with him, my distrust I was able to shed.
He was a very special teacher.
In fact, through his words and gestures and attention,
I experienced him as one would a preacher.
He gave me the tools, the guidance, and the needed structure
To discover and bring out my newfound ability
And to discover within me an appreciated agility.

This was a place which was sacred to me
As I slowly learned I was capable and able,
Where I could grow and to be completely separate from dad
And learn who I was and what was really me,
Even when he didn't agree.
This was a place I could feel free
To find my own independence.

My teacher teased out my talents
And brought out my soul for me to meet.
He had no other agenda than for me to be a dancer,
And through his teachings and his classes,
I found many of my own answers.

But there came a day in my upper teens when everything changed.
It seemed as though others got it, but I didn't have a clue.
He had expectations that were tacit.
Others had parents who got the memo and knew
Of what and how the next steps would be.
Unbeknownst to me,
He had expected me and my mom to know every facet.

Apparently, he expected me to move and perform,
To interview and travel to places to audition,
To go to a professional school and continue to grow and transform,
To perfect my craft and to teach and to dance,
To become a professional and to follow my ambition.

With my parents as well not having a clue,
And dad thinking dance was just showing off,
I, as a young woman, didn't even know it could be my due.
I hadn't enough confidence

To go out on my own,
And without a parent to support me,
To travel with me and have my back,
I began to think it was only a hobby
And was very aware of what I lacked.

If only I knew what he wanted.
What did I miss that my friends seemed to understand?
What if I could ask him questions and tell him I was totally lost?
But that didn't happen, and to me with great cost.
There was a sadness inside of me where I almost gave up
The dance that I loved and the belief in me and the relief it brought.
That sadness still has a place inside where it still resides.

Eventually, many years later,
I found my way back through another avenue.
I found another style of dance,
Which gave me and my muscular body another chance.
It was modern dance, not ballet,
Which became my style and my jewel.
I was able to take classes and to even get my masters.
To take chances until I became a professor in modern dances.
I became someone who taught and inspired others
To bring out their best and their latent talents.
I came full circle and became like my teacher, the man I admired.
He is still alive, although he is now long retired.
I never thanked him,
Nor do I think he knows the gift he gave me.
It is up to me to reach out to him,
To overcome my reticence,
Which I know is related to my lack of confidence,
And just say, "Thank you."

MY MOM

After my mom died,
I realized how she kept dad going and satisfied.
His ego so big and so needy,
She provided for his needs, which for her was a personal tragedy.
You might wonder about her.
I write as if she wasn't in the picture.
She was the one that was hard to capture.
I know she was depressed,
And living with dad she was daily oppressed.

Children were not her thing.
I think she found herself wanting,
And yet she had four.
Dad wanted four more.

As a result, she was anxious.
In her mothering she probably felt thankless.
Dad took her over.
It made her quite sober.
So disappear she would in her mind,
Not really hearing us in kind.
I believe she tried her best.
It sometimes being hard for her to even dress.
She dressed us in navy and beige,
Colors I hated at teen age.

At times, she was present,
And those rare times were transcendent.
I wish I knew my mom better

And that it was her, not dad, who wrote me the letters.
But I have her inside me,
And for me, it will have to suffice.
When I need my mom, I go to me for advice.

MY BUBBE

It was my Bubbe and my Zaydieman
That dad couldn't stand.
I loved them.
It was something I just couldn't understand.
What was it about them that had him so mean?
And I was supposed to hate them too.
It was Bubbe and Zaydieman and dad that I was in between.

My Bubbe it was who loved to dance,
Who taught me The Charleston and gave me a chance.
She took me to plays and out for ice cream.
She played and she sang and she taught me some songs.
At times, it was her who gave me self-esteem.
I couldn't understand how she could be so wrong.

It was Zaydieman who made me borscht.
It looked so strange at first; to eat it I was forced.
Who, when I was ill, brought me hot tea with lemon and honey,
Especially when my nose was runny.
Who made me, at Passover, matzah meal cakes,
Even though it was as early as daybreak,
And even let me put ketchup into his coffee,
Which he then pretended to drink up.

Be that as it may, I began to hold them with some caution.
I loved them, but soon, with her, I couldn't soften.

I was told that she cries and she lies
And with her, I couldn't always be allies.

She couldn't be believed,
And for that, she had to be deceived.

Maybe she did; maybe she did tell some lies.
But to me, she was soft and much love I received.

And towards the end it was hard, as she so badly needed her son.
She was so hurt by him
That it made her undone.

It was then that I saw what always was there.
Dad told lies and was so deceiving,
It was he—he was the one who couldn't be believed.
With him, it was I who was so naïve.

My Bubbe was who was there all the time,
Whose love was real and at times was sublime.
Who told me the truth,
Even in my youth,
And believed in me and told me I am a giver.
Who told me my first love was no good, even though he made me shiver.

My Bubbe was there, and it makes me sad.
I couldn't often be open to her because of my dad.
Yet I know in her heart, even from heaven,
She knows I love her and always have.

CLIMBING A MOUNTAIN:
A Hero's Journey

Climbing a mountain without a doubt,
Still just a kid, kicking about,
Not a care in the world,
Not one shred of doubt,
Hiking with my dad, so excited I could shout.

Past the riot of wildflowers—red, blue, and golden,
Up we went onward, mile after mile
To the frigid, clear running waters of fall after fall.
Quenching our thirst, resting our feet,
Emboldened to ascend the steep slope.
Becoming hungry, hoping some food would give our step hope.

Resting to eat until we ran out of snacks,
Onward we went carrying lighter backpacks
Over miles till we saw the tree line,
Now just fields and fields of gray boulders
Past the painted green pines and aspen.
After a few more hours,
We began dreaming of when our next bite would occur.
Imbued with thoughts and intent of a conquest
To help keep us going,
Our stomachs were grumbling, and our hunger was growing.
The next meal to come was still our unknowing.

As fate would have it,
Not so much later,
As we were jumping over and between the rocks,

There appeared in the distance some boys wearing blue.
Scouts they were, and all excited I got.
I jumped on ahead as if I just knew
That maybe they would have some food to share.
And they did, little red energy bars to fuel our tiring bodies.

So onward we went till we got towards the top.

It was then I got scared because I saw a storm brewing
Just as we made it close to the peak.
We were supposed to be down by the time the storm came.
There, right in front of me, was a cliff so steep, so straight up,
I got to stewing,
And attached to its side was a huge ice-cold cable
Running vertical to the top.
I started to doubt if I was truly able to climb that cable.
My dad had my older sister of only thirteen go first,
And she got stuck behind a large rock, unable to pull herself over.
On the way up behind her, I started to become unstable.
When I looked way down to the rock field below,
Fear took hold, which I tried to deny.
As my naked cold hands started to lose their traction,
I wanted to cry.
My brother of only eight came next after me.
Dad took the rear in fear for his young son becoming unsteady,
As he had an illness as an infant that left him off balance.
He had no care for my sister, who was not in shape nor able.
I started to slip and yelled out in distress.
If only my sister could move on ahead.
I used all my strength that I could possibly possess
To just hold on instead.
Why in the world did he have her go first

When I was one year younger and so much stronger?
The longer this lasted I felt worse and worse.
My fear had me scared like no other time ever.
Soon, just as I felt I might actually slip off,
I felt dad's hand touch my foot,
And in the magic of the moment, I believed dad's later story.
Dad told me I had let go and he was there behind me
As he then climbed over my brother still holding onto the cable,
Which then saved me from becoming fatal.
My dad did get there behind me; how, I don't know.
Holding on by one hand, he pushed up my sister,
And then I was able to shimmy up the cable.
At that point, I knew I hadn't let go,
But later this day, I wondered—had I let go or had I slipped?
All I know is that all it took was his touch to make me feel stable.
What really happened, I might never know.
He told the story of his saving me from dying.
Later, much later, I now know he was lying.
Wondering again later what else he was lying about,
But I was glad he was there as I hadn't fully let go.
By the next day, I became the fool who believed his story,
Blow by blow,
That I had let go while he somehow saved me.
That magical thinking to please him, I paid for dearly.

So, in a split second I was back against the rock,
And then next thing I knew, I had scrambled to the top.

We then all scrambled the rest of the way
To the top of the mountain,
Where all around, all I could see was fields below me,
So far below, small as could be,

With trees and trails and roads and such,
So far below, it made me feel excited and flush.
From miles away, I saw the storm coming quickly upon us.
Somehow, we made it before it was here,
But now we had to go, so we went on quickly nonplussed.
Suddenly, down we went to begin our descent.

We went down a different way where I slid down on my butt.
The way was so steep, I couldn't imagine staying on my feet.
Late it was becoming as the light was dimming,
As dad got us lost with no one else around.
We kept going forward for miles until we finally found
The trail that looked like the one we needed.

On past the boulders, till the fir trees were visible,
With the darkness impending,
I began to feel miserable.
I ran on down the last two miles.
Knowing the end of the climb was near, I couldn't stop smiling.
So proud was I to accomplish this feat,
I couldn't wait to get to the lodge and put up my feet.

Upon reaching the bottom, I was shocked by a crowd.
Apparently, our climb took us into the night,
And rangers and family were there waiting, shrouded by darkness.
At a loss to find us, they were in quite a fright.
I was so excited and exalted, I had no idea
That others would be waiting,
Frightened and wondering of our plight.

Getting back to the lodge, a meal was waiting,
And then I danced to the square dance late into the night.

By the next day, my dad took this story.
It became about him and his incredible feat.
He took over the story and made himself a hero.
He, who put us in danger all for his glory.
From then on, I felt small and truly a zero.
For he was the one who saved me from death
As I let go on the mountain while holding my breath.
And he was the hero, my savior, he who I could count on.
I was embarrassed and lost my power—that I could not discount.

It took me years to recover,
To feel more empowered
As I became clear with what I finally discovered—
That I was the hero and he was a fool
For putting us in danger because he wanted to.

Not a thought had he for all those who cared,
Who were back at the lodge not knowing what happened
To us on the mountain with him, as he imagined,
His need to be big, a hero, a man.

In my life-defining moment, I realized my stand,
By seeing myself becoming the woman I am.
The day became one of my great accomplishments,
As I successfully abolished the story of it being his glory.
I completed the climb. I did it. *I* did.
Strong and able and still only a kid!

BLIND

I have a sister who was born without hearing.
At times, I am sure she felt like disappearing.
My father played blind,
Which put my mother in a bind
As he pretended that everything was normal
Until my sister was almost two,
When her deafness he could no longer eschew.

She soon had an operation
Which ended one of the causations,
And suddenly, there was a little hearing.
Still needing an aid,
We moved for a special school, as dad was afraid.

She never learned to sign,
As dad was embarrassed
And needed for everything to be fine.
So she learned to read lips,
Which was definitely a trick
And allowed him to get a grip.

When we were at the dinner table,
Dad still wasn't able
To admit this made her feel unstable.
Instead of sitting in the middle
Where she could feel part of the family,
She sat at the end, which for her, was a calamity.
There, she couldn't hear
And be within our sphere,
So she had no choice but to disappear.

She grew up feeling apart,
Which broke her heart,
And so she was quiet.
As she followed dad's diet,
Words became an issue.
Self-expression a great fissure,
Making her feel more alone.

I never knew
Nor did I have a clue
All that she had been through.
So as I learned more,
We started to develop a good rapport.
And as we grew older,
Together we became bolder
To learn together and become more tender.
Not alone anymore as we continue to explore
What our life was like before.

When we were growing up,
We were kept at a distance.
This kept us from having each other for assistance.
Dad kept us separate
So for him we were desperate
And never learned how to really be sisters
Nor for each other to be good listeners.
But siblings we are,
And even with our quibbling,
I can honestly say how good it makes me feel to want to kiss her.

LIED TO

My blue eyes blinked.
It took only a split second,
And in that time,
Almost by design,
I missed a key clue,
And ever so suddenly I just knew
That I had been lied to.

When things don't make sense,
Even with, on their part, much finesse,
A tap of a finger on their nose,
A blink of their eye,
An expectation that I will comply,
I know I have been lied to.

I so badly want to believe,
And so I can be very naïve.
If I only blink my blue eyes,
I'm afraid I will be taken,
So metaphorically, I pinch myself
So that I will awaken.

MEMORIES

Traveling through my life,
I am struck by the strangeness of memory.
In my mind is a photo gallery,
And when I talk with old friends,
Their gallery is hard for me to comprehend.

My pictures have their own timeline.
Does it match theirs?
Often, that is hard to find.

Who is right and who is wrong?
Sometimes I just go along,
While in my mind, I am trying to recover
My old memories to rediscover
Lost pictures of my experiences,
Which can be both delicious and mysterious.

As I review the pictures from their eyes,
I take on all those that do apply,
And suddenly new memories appear,
Which feel quite queer.
Yet, seeing them from their sphere,
Old things, once lost, become suddenly clear.

Memory is a strange thing.
Sometimes they really sting.
And other times, I am excited about the old stories they bring.
Are your pictures true or are mine?
It really doesn't matter.
Maybe it is all by a divine design.

PART THREE: COMING UNDONE

NAÏVE

They say I can be quite naïve.
It comes from so badly wanting to believe.
I, who had something missing inside,
Maybe a hole where part of myself could reside,
Become susceptible to those who appear to be in charge,
Because I think they have the answer
To what inside me has been discharged.

When dad walked into the room,
With his need to be the One,
He took all the air and left me all alone,
And my own selves I shunned.
To make room for his needs,
I was the one who was ultimately deceived.

He taught me to get caught up in his words.
It was what he said that was true,
So please don't notice his actions,
For they don't match what he verbally espouses.
Like a magician with a slight of hand,
Don't look too close to review.

He was the ultimate deceiver,
And I was one of the intended receivers.
He hypnotized me with his command of English,
With one finger against his nose,
Looking very distinguished.
He then successfully guided me to relinquish
What I would have known had I trusted my senses.

This plowed through most of my defenses
And left me alone and vulnerable.

So naïve I became,
Believing in word and not deed.
Such is the nature of a cult leader.
At times, this was how dad could be the ultimate deceiver.

It is now my job and my job alone:
To fill my holes,
To know myself deep into my bones,
To recover trust in myself that became eroded,
And in turn, become again whole,
To learn to be vulnerable with others,
And to honor and feel in my gut
My needs.
It is others' actions and deeds that speak volumes,
And by trusting my gut reactions that within me sprout the seeds,
That, ultimately, is the demise of my naïve.

ON THE SURFACE

On the surface he could appear so...brilliant,
Loving, lyrical, caring, and crazy and intelligent.
And when he was hurt, he was so resilient,
But if it is true, he feels crossed.
Then, to him, you become his albatross.
His own ugly feelings he could not own,
So he put them on you,
And this way he could be his own boss.
His way with words so profound
That through them, he became renowned.
He could twist a meaning
To the way he was leaning
And make everything about how he saw them and was feeling.
And, of course, he was always right,
Making sure he was with all his wit and his might.
Don't become his enemy
Or see things through which he doesn't agree
Or even not be his acolyte.
He will make sure you are dimmed,
And he becomes the very bright light
At your expense, which can defy commonsense.
So those in his know who bow and kowtow
See things through his eyes and know he is right.
He is loving and kind and even quite funny,
Singing limericks and songs which are very punny.
While those who are stung become wrong and take flight,
With his words, he can destroy,
And in doing so, he takes such joy,
Never owning his part in his own selfish feelings.

On the surface, he is brilliant, loving, and kind,
But please never cross him.
He will turn you into the monster
That he feels he is inside and in kind.

WHITE COLLAR CRIMES

White collar crimes,
Dark sweatshirt grime.

Strong, honest, charming, bright, endearing.

User, believable, trusting.

Liar.

Ally, friend, father, teacher, mentor, guide, therapist.

White collar crimes,
Dark sweatshirt grime.

Baseball, coach, athlete.
Funny, punny.

Wooer, helper, leader.
Manipulator, betrayer.

White collar crimes,
Against human-atomy.

And we believed...
Until we didn't.

White collar crimes,
Dark sweatshirt grime.

White collar crimes,
Dark sweatshirt grime.

THE LOST CARNY

Come bare your souls;
I'll take your money.
What's the matter,
Can't you trust me, honey?

Like a carny and a bum,
A truth-sayer, a wizard,
I'll take your money.
Can't you trust me, honey?

Say what you will.
I'll say what I will.
Who do you trust?
Come and trust me, honey.

Try as I might,
Conned with such fright.
Come on, I want your money.
I'll cry and I'll fight.
You know that I'm right.
Now give up the fight.
I'll cry till you do.
I'm telling the truth.
So what's the matter,
Can't you trust me, honey?

FROM BEHIND THE CURTAIN

Suddenly, when dad was about seventy,
I noticed a deepening of his anxiety.
Most of his life, he hid it so well
That when it became so evident,
I, at first, had trouble believing it.

He got lost coming home,
Which mom kept most secret
Until it became much more frequent.
He became obsessed with money,
Trying every scam he could find,
Attempting to talk us into them blind.
Believing them himself, he truly was at sea.
Unfunny it became, believe you me.
He soon lost his car, lost his home, lost his money.

If that wasn't the worst, he then lost his words.
He, who was articulate and relied on his mind,
Who could talk anyone into anything that soon dropped behind.
And then it was,
I saw what was there.

Just a little old man, he walked out from the curtain.
It was then I could see
The man who he was,
Not who I wanted him to be.

Before that day, I knew I was certain
That my dad was the greatest, the funniest, the best,

The man I could trust with my heart, with my life,
Who I thought told the truth, which I held to my breast.
It was then that I knew that wasn't so true.
He was a little old man, a little boy I could see through.
A grown little boy who was aptly named Roy.
He wasn't the king, the man with a doctor degree,
Or even a man who had much integrity.
He wasn't the greatest, the best, or the funniest.
He wasn't a man that I could really trust.
Away from the curtain, I saw who he was—
A little lost boy whose mind hid his weakness,
Which no longer could hide his strong hidden bleakness.
And I saw the true person he was as he stood.
The man I once saw as the man who was so good
Is a flawed boy who wanted us to believe that he could.

FORGIVE

To dad's parents, he was mean,
Whether he was seven, seventy, or even a teen.
He couldn't forgive.
To him, that was a foreign word,
And one that was the opposite of live.

For him, he believed in his heart
He was abandoned and lied to,
And never any love for them could he retrieve.

His work was all about going deep inside
And healing the holes that had been left behind.
And help them he did,
But forgiveness was a concept
In which he didn't believe and so was inept
And was not ever able to help them with,
No matter his skill as a wordsmith.

When his father came to town from Chicago to visit
To be with us for the Seder,
Dad needed to lead and fought tooth and nail,
For leading was something for which he would never give up
And he wouldn't fail.
"Over my dead body," he might say.
For him, it could not be any other way.

Zaydieman, his dad, had to concede,
Or I should say, secede,
For when dad felt hate,

There was never any debate,
And Zaydieman was one he would never forgive.

To forgive, in dad's mind, was to give up something that is yours
And not to work with and transform energy and beliefs that hurt us.
To do so would not be to heal, but to deform.

You see, dad never could let go of
Anything at all where he felt he was right.
Then he would be in a place where he felt he had to fight.
That was a plight that was with him till the end.
For to him, if he wasn't right, he might as well be dead.

COMING UNDONE

This is a story of dad coming undone.

Thumb drum Thumb drum.

And suddenly, to dad, money became a thing,
Before which it was a prayer and a wing.
He said, "Money was there to spend."
And he did; he spent everything he had.
So he tried every fad
In a hurry to grow wealth,
And he was stealthily and steadily had.

Thumb drum thumb drum.

He went to Amsterdam alone
And was shown a bank lined with money,
Given a check to take home.
He felt the world was his and so sunny,
Never realizing the money was funny.
The check was a fake.
But he was friends with his scammers,
And there was no way they would "take" him, would they?
But he was left in emotional tatters.

Thumb drum thumb drum.

Then they took him to Paris,
And there he was wined and dined,
Simultaneously taking every one of his dimes.

Thumb drum thumb drum.

So he took to "borrowing" money
From his friends, family, and foe.
He borrowed and begged and cajoled,
Promising a large return on their investments
From which they were all divested.
He begged from his daughter,
And that did nothing but taught her
To never give in to him ever again.

Thumb drum thumb drum.

He borrowed money from his son
To pay for his home, for he had none.
But he didn't pay the mortgage; he paid the scammers,
And then they lost their house and became undone.

Thumb drum thumb drum.

He seemed to have no remorse.
He seemed to treat hurting others as a matter of course.
He took and he took and he paid and he paid.
In the end, he lost everything
And there was nothing and no one from which
      he could gain aid.

Thumb drum thumb drum.

After we moved him into a facility,
My sister and I went to clean out his place
      with great humility,
And in every drawer, we found thousands of money grams
To which he paid out to every damn sham.

Thumb drum thumb drum.

He wanted to leave a legacy of wealth
And went about it all wrong.
But what he didn't realize
Was that we were all really strong.
We didn't need his wealth.
We all had our health.
His obsession was all about himself.

Thumb drum.

LOSING HIS MIND

Then there came the time
When he got tangled in white collar crime.
I ask, *Was it his mind that had begun to unravel?*
His words also disappeared and became all scrambled.

And then one day, I got a call.
I could tell he was really enthralled.
"Come meet us for dinner.
We have become winners."

He went to Amsterdam as part of a big international scam.
These people, they befriended him.
He gave them his trust,
And then he gave them all his and others' money—
Family, friends, and patients alike.
All the fake money and friends became his honeys.

With this began a new trend.
From then on, the scammers were his friends.
Nigerian, European, and even a trip to Paris they financed.
They had to clean the money that dad took from others in advance.
He took from his friends, his patients, and even his colleagues.
Promising them much money,
Their trust in him made them believe.
In return, he was out of his league.

He was very sincere,
But soon it all did disappear.
He lost it all, lost everything.

He lost his house and his car,
And then he sold everything more.

My brother lent him money to keep his house.
Next thing I know, he and mom were kicked out.
This was all for his legacy, which was really a lunacy.

His mind is without words,
His trust and judgment in others impaired.
He was left with nothing,
His mind all a crumble, and he wasn't a dime spared.
He took from others as he himself was taken.
From this, there was no way he could awaken.

White collar crime, all for a dime.
Ah, what a time it was.
His mind now lost and a jumble.

OFF THE HOOK

When I speak to people who are in dad's camp,
No matter what transpired and what he took,
It seems that they let him off the hook.

Except one old friend, who has now passed,
Wondered aloud one day,
"How is it you all have grown and not crashed?"

In fact, it was hard to grow and to mature.
Overcoming his allure certainly did make us unsure.
I became a late bloomer,
Through years of therapy and self-help,
Even trying healthy diets of tofu and kelp.

And amazing as it is, people let him off the hook.
His wise and brilliant counsel,
His mind full of helpful insights,
His heart, if not hurt, full and open,
He gifted many also with fun delights.

No matter what he did or who and how he hurt,
If you were in his camp,
Many let him off the hook.

I was asked recently if I loved him as they certainly did.
My answer surprised me in a way.
I too, in some ways, let him off the hook.
There was so much I experienced, I could write a book.
My answer is I love him in some ways and always will.
In other ways, I don't, and never can.

THE MASTER OF PROJECTION

He confided in me in the end.
No longer did he feel the need to defend,
After mom had died
And after all that he tried.
Dad realized, at root, he was a bad man.
For all of his own fantasies and dreams,
He was a master of projection.
To all those for whom he couldn't bother,
Especially his mother and his father,
He was a master of obsession.
We were not his confections.
He knew it in his bones,
And he felt it in his jones.
His fantasies he projected,
Afraid of being rejected,
And he even dealt with them in his profession.
Mom wouldn't be waiting for him when he died,
And for that, he cried and cried and cried.

PART FOUR:
MY DANCE

INDEPENDaNCE

Then it was time for me to go to college.
You could say it was to collect knowledge.
Why I went carried no thought.
It was just what everyone sought, or you might even say bought.

My first choice I was denied.
And yes, when I heard, I certainly cried.
Afterwards, I was a bit lost,
But find a college I did, at a personal cost.
When I arrived, I found I was very ill-advised.
Sad and lonely,
I looked forward each week for dad to phone me.

Phone me he did,
And love letters he wrote.
Maybe they were to help keep me afloat,
But love letters they were.

Were they meant to woo,
Like the song he would sing, "A Bicycle Built for Two."
Confused and in a trance,
Do I move towards indepen~dance?
Or do I move towards pleasing,
Which would give me much grieving?
How do I please him and me?
Is that even possible?
Is it something that is crossable?

So I fell into a pit,
Where I felt extremely split.
Depression they called it.

So home I went back to,
To the scene of the crime,
To try to find a way to heal, which takes time.
I needed to be close to dad but in my own pad,
In order to find my way out of this dyad.

It was then that I met the man for whom I took a chance
And I began the journey towards my dance—
Towards my independence.

FIRST ROMANTIC LOVE: SAGA

I was nineteen and
Just a young woman,
First falling in love.

I saw first his eyes,
And my body responded.
One thing I know, my body never lies.

His eyes framed by his glasses,
Round and in style,
His eyes met mine,
And I shivered in his classes.

At the head of the stage,
Ready to teach,
His eyes met mine.
My reaction instinctive and one not to gauge.
My age not an issue
As I shivered and jumped.
I really was quite stumped by my reaction.

The class he co-taught was The Alexander Technique,
One which is truly quite unique.
He places his hands gently around my neck.
His hands give a direction,
To give my body a gentle correction.
Afraid I was
That he would then know—
My body would jump and my reaction would show.

But onward I went, to class after class.
Hungry both for correction and connection,
As I was a dancer.
The class's intention an answer
To the knots in my muscles,
Accumulated over years of dancing,
An extremely long tussle to finding relief.

The class was designed,
Through guidance, to realign
And to help me to move smoothly throughout my spine.

At the time, he was married—
A fact that made me quite wary.
But onward I went, for the class and the feeling,
And that was something for me that was very scary.

And one day it happened, one day after class.
We stayed together after all had departed.
We talked and we walked and then it started.

I didn't feel judged.
I didn't feel shame.
All I know is that I felt this incredible flame.

It wasn't just me.
He felt it too.
We talked and we walked.
We hugged and we kissed.
This was an opportunity I didn't want to miss.

I wanted to love but was told I was unable.
Dad told me I was not able
To love anyone, from the time in my cradle.
And I found out here that it was just a fable.

So we kissed and we kissed,
And Tuesdays was our night,
For his wife had to work, and that night—for us—just felt so right.

I was a virgin.
It was my secret.
I couldn't tell him, for I was embarrassed.
I thought maybe I was just his current whim,
So on we went through the semester.
He didn't tell his wife,
And we let our secret fester,
Til soon it was time
And she was finally told.
He moved in with me,
But we didn't really feel free.

Believe in me he did,
And he helped to rekindle my career.
He steered me back to dance,
And I had no more fear.

To Nebraska we went for a summer workshop,
To learn from his teacher
At the months long feature.
Consisting mostly of dancers and actors and singers,
We were at a Fraternity House of artists, not amateurs.

Sharing a house with friends and seekers,
We split up in groups to cook and to clean,
And there, I found this man, my first love, could be very mean.

Just like my dad, in public, put down my mom
He too blew me up and, in public, put me down.
He was not fooling around,
And it made me feel like I wanted to hide and to drown.

But learn I did, and my body began to flourish.
It was there that I also felt nourished.

We drank fresh milk directly from the cow,
And did farm work that time allowed.
We had classes and made friendships
And even were able to take short little trips.

In private, he was different.
> He was loving and kind
>> And inspired me with his belief in me and his mind.

We made love and we fought.
> It was all love could be,
>> Or so I thought.

Another shadow soon showed its face.
I did my best to put it in its place,
But he had a roaming eye, and that became clear.
I tried so hard, and failed, to deny.

It reminded me of dad,
Who had affairs he hid so well
With both friends and patients.
And now, with my love,
It was sometimes more than I could bear.

But ahead we plowed,
Despite the silent cloud.
To marriage was our bent.
To this, I gave my total assent.

A counselor was suggested to us.
This, I knew would be helpful and I couldn't contest.
Soon with the counselor's help and after much consideration,
The marriage plans we had decided were best to be arrested.

Soon it was my graduation
And time for another Nebraska situation.
He was there for the summer, and I was in St Louis.
I couldn't wait for us to be reunited.

He was there acting in a summer theatre,
Where he could have fun and keep practicing his art.
We rejoined at our teacher's house,
And I felt like there, in public,
He treated me like I was little more than a mouse.

He held me at arm's distance,
I believe to express to me his need to be free,
But it surprised me and made me feel extremely crappy.

The next day we met at a park.
He wanted to walk and to talk.
When we started to walk, he said something
Which broke me apart.

"I fell in love," he said.
With those words, I screamed and quickly ran ahead.
I was filled with such terrible dread,
My reaction completely instinctive.
At the time, I had no thought and no preparation.

Love is forever,
I thought.
Those were words and feelings I had bought.
How could he do this to me?
In my mind, I had no choice but to flee.

After me he chased,
Ignoring my need for my sacred space.
He tackled me to the ground gently,
And then held me both feelingly and absently.

Afterwards, everything was changed,
Inwardly and out,
Yet we went limping along with everything rearranged,
Sometimes together and sometimes estranged.

I went to Ohio,
In some ways feeling quite spent.
But I went there to dance,
And even through the internal chaos I was experiencing,
My dance was enhanced.

I got my masters in dance
While off in the distance, he still held me in a trance.
He was living in San Francisco
And me in Columbus,
Keeping me entangled through late night phone calls
And some quiet evening bawls.

Then one day, it happened.
        It was time, although I was extremely saddened.

I left him.
It was over.
For two straight weeks I cried.
Such grief was very hard for me to abide.
But leave him I did,
For now and forever.
My first love, for now and forever,
Was finally over.

ENDINGS AND BEGINNINGS

My marriage is ending,
And I know I haven't transcended
All the issues between us,
As I still feel such disgust,
Not just with him, but with both of us.

He is so competitive regarding our son
And still needing my full attention.
This I can't give,
For it is my son who needs me to live.

I have this little boy
Who brings me so much joy.
With my husband, I can't share
All my cares, feelings and daily affairs.
But if I don't find a way,
I know, in this marriage I can't stay.

I want what's best for my son.
In divorce, there is no such thing as who won.
I am doing my absolute best—
That, I can honestly attest.
No matter how much I am stressed,
With my son, I am greatly impressed.

To guide and protect,
To teach and to love:
As my words go to god above,
That is what I vow
And I truly hope to endow.

All that I nurture,
And as a single mother, I will begin the journey to juggle
Both my work as a mother and a doctor,
And that is a wonderful struggle.

I slowly build my practice,
And at the same time, I take my son to practice
All the skills and the sports
Of his interests that I can support.

The struggle is real
But one of such joy.
I will do anything I can for this wonderful little boy.

MY INDIVIDUATION

I embarked on my individuation,
    Not without any trepidation.
It was quite a task,
    And it was all I asked,
    To find who I am
    And for that to be my jam.

For me, the question was:
    How can I be myself while in relationships
    And it be enough for me to be my own courtship?
The answer required from me a very long journey.

To engage with others and see them realistically
    And not just as I would have done then,
    Which was mystically—
To see the ordinary and the extraordinary
    And to create the gate to bring them together.

To do so involved I investigate my roots,
    A deep subject where I needed my mud boots
    To trek through the muck to get me unstuck,
And to know and to love
    The self I have come to respect,
    To individuate as well as create myself with another—
    Deep, real, connected, and direct.

MOTHERHOOD

I was afraid to be a mother—
Afraid I would either be absent or I would smother,
Like dad who gave too much,
Which in turn, gave us such a crutch.
For he was the only one who knew the way
And did it so that we would stay.
Or like my mom,
Who was extremely depressed,
And with us was so, so stressed.

I felt either unseen or too needy
To be there for my child.
It seemed like it would be a wild ride.
I certainly wasn't a child bride.

A balance I needed to find—
That would certainly ease my mind.
To be there for me and for him,
To be in the middle,
As happy and beautiful as a fiddle.

To do that would quell,
That would very well dispel,
The fears that live within me.
To live and to mother in balance—
That is all, in a nutshell.

MARRIAGE NUMBER TWO

Marriage number two was nothing like Mr. Magoo.

My blinders were off.

In fact, I wanted to see, to know what I was getting into.
This was something I needed to view.

Clearly, I had a son to consider.
I wanted this dearly.

To love, to cherish, and to lightly hold,
In this case now, I needed to be bold.

I learned love can come easily,

But it needs to be held delicately.

It is easily broken and not so repaired.
This was now something I needed to dare.

He was my son's karate teacher.
I watched him teach from the gym's bleacher.

In awe I was with his skill and prowess.
If I couldn't see that, I would be amiss.

The kids loved him there, teaching in that gym.
A role model I was looking for,
And I think I found him on that floor.
He was also attractive; that, I couldn't ignore.

Soon it was we began to date,
And I knew I wanted to know him more.

We dated slowly, as there was my boy involved,
And slowly we let our relationship evolve.

Here was a man who stood up for himself,
Who never let dad get in our way,
Who was his own man
From the time we began.

Our relationship grew and soon we married.
Over time, I learned to not keep my true self buried.

Please him I did, but I pleased myself too.
I really didn't marry Mr. Magoo.

Slowly my voice began to get stronger.
We grew together and our love grew as well.
Through hard times and good times,
We really could tell.

He loved me enough, even to learn tango.
He loved me through my internal crisis.
We loved each other, even when we felt self-righteous.

This time, my eyes were open.
I married a different man.
He's not Mr. Magoo.
And nor am I.

TRANSCENDaNCE

Back when I was growing up, breakfast with dad was great.
It was also a way he gave mom a break.
For me, Sunday breakfast became habitual,
One with the reverence of a ritual.
It reminds me of dad,
The good and the bad,
And a time to be with family and friends.
Here, I can pass on the love from my heart
And make this a time where the negative transcends,
Where the fun and the stories,
As beautiful as morning glories,
Become fertilizer for our future trends.
We can take this template
And rid it of anger and hate,
So we can pass on the best of our traits.
We can toast our old host,
And we can say hello to his ghost.
And here we can also create
The legacy he so badly wanted to initiate.
And in its place is our very own dance,
Our very own dance of transcendence.

TRIBUTE

He was a flawed man.
A friend called him an imperfect guru.
I wouldn't say that,
But I certainly saw him as being a bit askew.
He was my father and, at times and places, wonderful.
He made many mistakes which impacted me and hurt me.
The worst of all was what he did to be my all powerful.

You might think I didn't love my dad,
But I did.
This book of poems might even be considered a tribute,
Even though, at times, it sounds like a rebuke.
And it is, in its way.
I guess you could say it is my turn to have my say;
He certainly had plenty of his.

Dad said we all have our fault lines and blind spots.
That is true.
This book is about him, and it's about me too.

When we grow up, it's our job to forgive.
This is where he was always a fugitive.
His parents he faulted.
He never forgave them and always, from them, felt assaulted.
So he, in vengeance, returned the favor.
That was his own very unique flavor which he never outgrew.

But for me, it is different.
I always wanted to see and not be blind,

To see the truth I couldn't keep hiding from.
For you know, we are the children of our own kind.
I wouldn't be here if it weren't for them.
They are my parents, my very own brethren.

I chose to grow up, to see, to be my own person.
To do so meant I couldn't be my own desertion.
I love my dad and always did.
When I was little, he was my superman, my all.
From that height, for me to grow up,
He had to have a great fall.
That is why it was so hard to see
What he tried so hard to hide—
His anger and rage,
Which tainted all he clutched and all he touched.

But I choose to grow up, to love, and to forgive.
I see him now through compassionate eyes.
For it was because of him—the good, the bad, and the lies—
That made me who I am now
And all that allows.
With friends, allies, mentors, teachers, and family to guide me,
I have me, and I am mostly free and have my own independence,
Free from his interference.
In a way, this is a gift he gave me,
And I know it makes him proud
To see me do what in life he couldn't.

POSSIBILITIES

When I think about who and what I want to be,
Why in the world would I base it on what once was?
That only keeps me entrapped,
When really, I want to be free.
If I let go of my old stories,
I become open to many possibilities.

Once I do, I feel such relief.
I have a feeling of floating.
My foundation is just so different,
There is even a slight sense of disbelief.
The change is not insignificant.
What is truly amazing
Is realizing that I could have done it at any time,
If only I knew that I could.

It doesn't mean I forget what happened.
It doesn't mean I want or had a different family.
It's like I have a different map,
One which leads to divergent relationships from which I can tap.
And suddenly, one day, I awake
And realize what it is I want to leave and what I want to take.
From there, I can ask,
Why in the world would I hold onto those old beliefs and stories
When I could go forward, unentrapped by my past,
And feel such a sense of relief and freedom
Transpiring, with a sense of possibilities.

EPILOGUE: WHAT A PICTURE IS WORTH

My parents on their honeymoon.

In the wagon: my older sister, my younger sister, and me.

My dad played ball into his seventies.

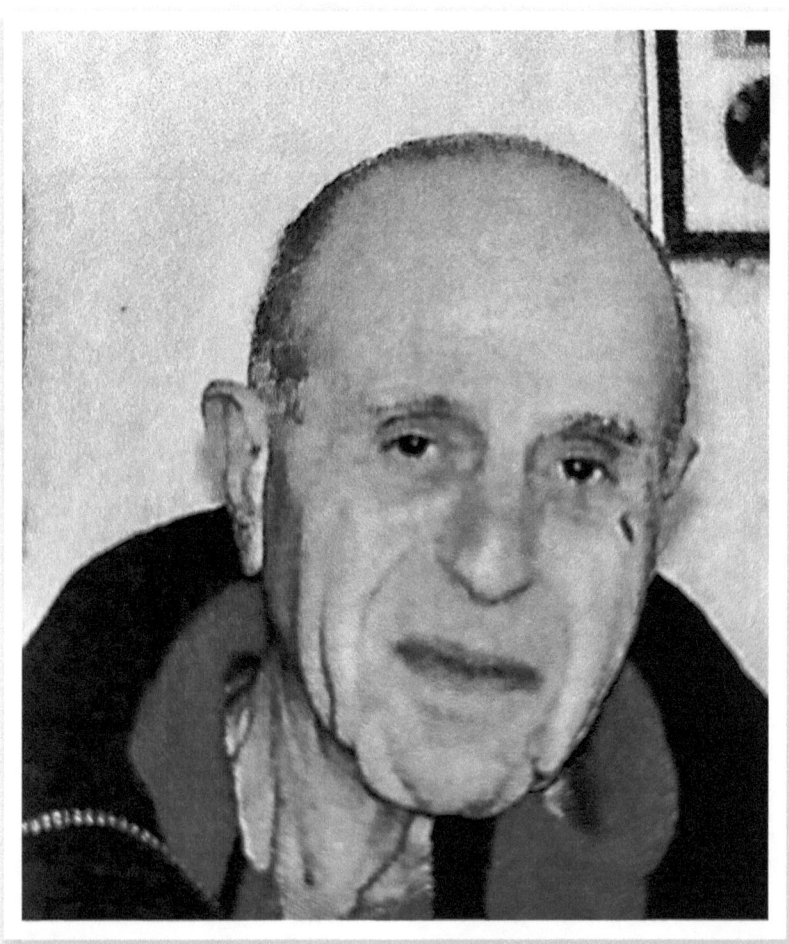

My dad as an older man.

REVISITING MY FIRST LOVE

I am rendezvousing again with my first, or should I say, second love? My father will always be my first.

No, this love isn't a person—it's ballet. I've started dancing again at the young age of seventy. It has been almost forty years since I last stepped into a ballet studio. When I whirled around as a child, dad didn't approve and made known his thought that dance was showing off.

Here I am, and in some ways, feeling like a child again.

Preparing to go to my first class in so many years, I have to confront anxiety about dancing in front of mirrors and people, as my body is now older, fuller, and shaped differently. Dad had made me extremely self-conscious about my figure. No longer do I have a waist of twenty inches. As a young dancer, I experienced judgment regarding my body shape and weight, not just from my father, as I have always had a muscular build on top of being five feet, one inch. Yes, I add that one inch! Now carrying twenty pounds more than my dancing weight, I am about to dance again and reenter the dance culture I once was part of. I have to empty my mind of all these judgments.

My first step is not a relevé, an arabesque, or even a plié—it is entering a dancewear store to purchase a leotard and tights. Trust me, I am not heavy. I am of medium build and toned and found myself having to stuff my average form into a large leotard. No longer are leotards crafted of ultrasoft, stretchy fabric. No, they are not so luxe. Rather, they use a stiff, inflexible material to shape and even out our little curves and bulges. They are mass-produced to try to make us look—by some ephemeral standard—"sexy."

Okay, I think, *I can do this. I just want to dance again. I have nothing to prove to myself or to anyone.* Once I enter the classroom, I feel at home again. *I know this. I love this.*

Once a dancer, always a dancer.

I took a deep, easy breath.

Now comes the hard work of getting into dance shape again. Reteaching my hips to open and turn out without compromising the integrity of my knees. Learning my new body and its capabilities at this age is interesting and fulfilling. What can I do, and what can't I, and what might I again be able to do are all questions I am learning and loving. The movements and exercises, remembered, feel as good as they hurt and ache.

My muscles and joints stretch and lubricate for barre exercises. My cells work to remember how to *pull* up and out of my hips. That is dance terminology meaning how to stand on one leg, on my toes, and not sink into the hips. Staying on top of my sacred temple requires incredible strength. After years of playing racquetball, doing martial arts, jogging, doing Pilates, yoga, working with a personal trainer—all good things— none of which ever felt or proved as hard as this ballet barre.

Seeing and experiencing again this marvelous and elegant training as an older woman with a myriad of workout experiences to fall back on, I know this is the best strengthening and lengthening workout there is. Dancers are elegant, elite athletes. And all elite athletes, in one way or another, dance.

So here I stand, in first position, in a beginning adult ballet class, older by thirty years than the other oldest dancer in the class, and I am in love again. In the mirror, I watch these other women and one man struggling and enjoying learning. I enjoy watching them step and leap into the challenge of teaching their bodies these difficult movements. I see them fall in love with ballet and also sprout a desire to get better fast. I know from experience, there is no "fast" in this equation. Ballet technique takes work, patience, persistence, and being in tune with our bodies, their abilities, and their limitations.

I watch how they dress for class, how each one tries to cover up the part of their body which they feel least fond of, and to accentuate the parts they prefer. It is its own beauty contest. Part of what every dancer deals with is the fact that unlike writing or painting or sculpting, *dancers are our own canvas*. We are representing ourselves, yes, and we are also expressing our art through our bodies and our movements. So how we look is important, although not always in the way dancers obsess about looks. *And not in the way I used to.*

Another lovely aspect of this go-around is: I am here strictly for fun, enjoyment, feeling good in my body/mind, stretching my boundaries, and relishing camaraderie with other like-minded souls.

It is freeing to have nothing to prove. I'm in it only for myself. I'm embracing this second love of mine now, not as a rebound, and not to prove anything to my first. I remember so clearly the years of ambition and competition and trying to be thin enough to fit in a body that was not then, not now, and not in this lifetime, a ballet body. In each movement, there is healing from the false accusation that I was ever showing off.

Our class has been asked to be part of a whole studio performance where our teacher, a professional dancer herself, choreographs a three-minute routine for us. I really don't want to perform, but as our class is small, and we are a team of sorts, I have agreed. We shall each wear a lavender sleeveless tutu in tulle. I am not sure it's a great look for an older woman with crepey skin.

Making peace with this, I get to witness myself from the point of view of, "Who wants to look at an old woman on stage dancing?" or—"Who wants to be inspired and motivated by watching an old woman keep up and dance with younger dancers?"

I choose the latter.

I am, after all, a therapist's daughter.

My father couldn't tell how essential ballet was for my life. This performance art based on infinitely more than pink, satin toe shoes became my therapy. And through it, I am able to notice what my father didn't see: the way it becomes me.

DANCE IS LIFE

Living and feeling and seeing and knowing
Feeling deep in my body, looking for messages
Nuances prod me to the depths of curiosity and understanding

Being...in my body
Developing resilience, elasticity, alignment
Overcoming and journeying through physical and emotional blockages

Dance offers the meaning of life all in the discovery of self
Discipline, vibration, creativity
Curiosity
Velocity
Sensuality through moving through the movement
Deeply regarding and understanding self through movement
Watching others courageously exploring their very beings
Through the vehicle of dance

At the barre
Standing tall
Aligning up through our hips
Feeling length through our toes and fingertips
Adjusting our balance
Stretching to our limits
Discovering the parts of us that inhibit
Bending our knees aligned over our toes
Opening our hips and widening our internal range
Up on the balls of our feet
Our hips both open and extended
As we lift one leg and bend the other
Maintaining the poise of our balance as we intended

Such beauty and grace
Hard work and surrender
Learning ourselves so fiercely and tender
In awe of our strength, our weaknesses too
Always striving to improve both inward and out
Learning to experience, appreciate and love our unique groove

Dance teaches us about life and love and belonging
We are part of a system starting with us and beyond
It is a pathway for a new world dawning
Let us not forget we are all part of a whole
Appreciating life, art, love, beauty and pain
It is a pathway to love us all and let it not be in vain.

ABOUT THE AUTHOR

After her first career as a dancer and teacher of ballet and modern dance, Gail Cloud, DC, realized that she wanted a career more service-oriented. She chose a practice that kept her dancing for many years—chiropractic work. Today Gail is a practicing chiropractor and an Inherited Trauma facilitator, working with somatic healing. She is also an astrologer, focusing on our growth and evolving selves, what gets in our way, and what strengths we possess to help us with our process.

Gail began writing this memoir in 2020, and through writing, discovered that using poetry was the best way for her to express her thoughts and feelings with such a personal and vulnerable subject. When not writing, she is walking with her dog, continuing her learning, enjoying time with her friends and husband, and has even started taking ballet lessons again.

www.bodypresencing.com

PUBLISHER'S NOTE

Thank you for your readership and the opportunity to serve you.
If you would like to share this book, here are some ways:

REVIEWS
Write an online book review

GIVING
Gift this book to friends, family, and colleagues

BOOK CLUBS
Read it with a group of colleagues or friends

EVENTS
Invite the author to be speaker for your organization
Email: info@citrinepublishing.com

BULK ORDERS
Email: sales@citrinepublishing.com

CONTACT
Call +1-828-585-7030 or email:
info@citrinepublishing.com

We appreciate your book reviews, letters, and shares.

www.ingramcontent.com/pod-product-compliance
Lightning Source LLC
Chambersburg PA
CBHW060530080526
44586CB00012B/693